SCIENCE KIDS
Life Cycles
Chickens

Ruth Daly

www.av2books.com

LET'S READ

AV²
BY WEIGL™

ADDED VALUE • AUDIO VISUAL

Go to **www.av2books.com**, and enter this book's unique code.

BOOK CODE

N95445

AV² by Weigl brings you media enhanced books that support active learning.

AV² provides enriched content that supplements and complements this book. Weigl's AV² books strive to create inspired learning and engage young minds in a total learning experience.

Your AV² Media Enhanced books come alive with...

Audio
Listen to sections of the book read aloud.

Video
Watch informative video clips.

Embedded Weblinks
Gain additional information for research.

Try This!
Complete activities and hands-on experiments.

Key Words
Study vocabulary, and complete a matching word activity.

Quizzes
Test your knowledge.

Slide Show
View images and captions, and prepare a presentation.

... and much, much more!

Published by AV² by Weigl
350 5th Avenue, 59th Floor New York, NY 10118
Websites: www.av2books.com   www.weigl.com

Library of Congress Control Number: 2014941062

ISBN 978-1-4896-1326-4 (hardcover)
ISBN 978-1-4896-1327-1 (softcover)
ISBN 978-1-4896-1328-8 (single user eBook)
ISBN 978-1-4896-1329-5 (multi-user eBook)

Printed in the United States of America in North Mankato, Minnesota
1 2 3 4 5 6 7 8 9 0 18 17 16 15 14

052014
WEP220514

Project Coordinator: Jared Siemens
Art Director: Terry Paulhus

Weigl acknowledges Getty Images as the primary image supplier for this title.

SCIENCE KIDS
Life Cycles
Chickens

CONTENTS

4

All birds begin life, grow, and make more birds. All birds will die in the end. New birds grow up to take their place. This is a life cycle.

6

Chickens are farm birds. All birds have feathers, a beak, and wings. Chickens can not fly very far.

A baby chicken is born when it breaks out of an egg. It uses its beak to make small holes in the shell. Then the baby chicken pushes its way out.

Baby chickens are called chicks. Chick feathers are wet and sticky at first. The feathers soon dry. These feathers are called down.

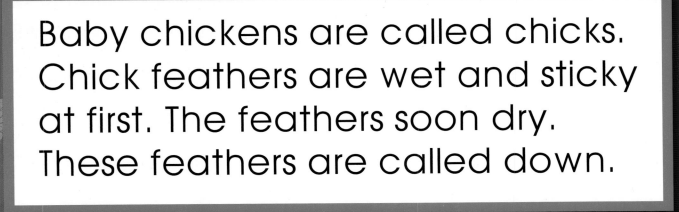

Down is yellow and fluffy. Down helps keep chicks warm.

Young chicks eat small plants and insects. Chicks grow very fast. The males are called cockerels. The females are called pullets.

13

A cockerel grows into a rooster. Roosters have brightly colored feathers. Pullets grow into hens.

Hens and roosters can be parents in the adult stage of the life cycle.

Hens can lay eggs when they are about six months old. Hens lay their eggs in nests. Hens can only lay one egg at a time.

Eggs have hard shells with yolk inside. Yolk is food for the chick to eat before it is born.

18

A hen sits on her eggs for 21 days. She does this to keep them warm. This is called brooding.

A hen can lay about 300 eggs in a year.

There are more than 100 kinds of chickens. Each kind has different colored feathers. Chicks get their feather colors from their parents.

Life Cycles Quiz

Test your knowledge of chicken life cycles by taking this quiz. Look at these pictures. Which stage of the life cycle do you see in each picture?

adult   chick
newborn   parent

KEY WORDS

Research has shown that as much as 65 percent of all written material published in English is made up of 300 words. These 300 words cannot be taught using pictures or learned by sounding them out. They must be recognized by sight. This book contains 74 common sight words to help young readers improve their reading fluency and comprehension. This book also teaches young readers several important content words, such as proper nouns. These words are paired with pictures to aid in learning and improve understanding.

Page	Sight Words First Appearance
4	a, all, and, end, grow, in, is, life, make, more, new, place, take, the, their, this, to, up, will
7	are, can, far, farm, have, not, very
8	get, it, its, of, out, small, then, uses, way, when
11	down, helps, keep, soon, these
12	eat, long, plants, young
15	be, into
16	about, at, before, food, for, hard, it, old, one, only, time, with
19	days, does, her, on, she, them, year
20	different, each, from, get, has, kinds, than, there

Page	Content Words First Appearance
4	birds, life cycle
7	beak, chickens, feathers, wings
8	baby, egg, holes, shell
10	chicks
12	cockerels, females, insects, males, pullets
15	hens, parents, rooster
16	months, nests, yolk
20	color